# I WANT TO LEAVE THIS BOOK!

Written by Richard David Lawman Illustrated by Katie Williams

This first edition published in the United Kingdom in 2019 by WatAdventure Publishing.

The characters that occur in this book are works of fiction and are used metaphorically to explain the broader subject matter, they are not references to single, specific individuals but to larger groups of people, movements and thoughts.

The moral rights of Richard David Lawman as the author and Katie Williams as the illustrator have been asserted.

This book was printed by Charlesworth Press, UK on sustainably forested paper.

© WatAdventure Publishing Ltd.

All rights reserved.

For Mum and Dad - RDL
For Ann, Audrey, Howard and Tom - KW

It was already the fourth page of this book and Sirius and Jiblets were waiting for the story to start.

"What's going to happen?" said Jiblets.
"I hope this story is going to be an adventure to space…

With cowboys…

Riding dinosaurs…

From the future…

But it's all in your mind!"

Sirius chuckled, "I don't think that's likely, Jiblets.

I hope this story will be a mystery, perhaps. A period-drama, maybe…
And involving lots of sitting down on comfy armchairs."

"Ugh. That sounds **boring!**" moaned Jiblets.

"Well yours sounds **preposterously ludicrous!**" snapped Sirius.

"Well, in that case," said Jiblets,

# "I WANT TO LEAVE THIS BOOK!"

"Leave this book? Why?" said Sirius.

"Nothing is happening!" said Jiblets.

"The words are **rubbish!**

The pictures are **terrible!**

Am I really supposed to be **orange?**

I don't even get a say in what happens.
I just have to do as I'm told."

"Jiblets, we're lucky to be in a book at all!" said Sirius.

"Feel the quality of that paper.
You don't get that in most books.
Look how it brings the colours out!
And look at the **quality of the lettering.**
Magnificent.

This will be a really, really, really good story,
**I'm sure of it.**"

"We're already on the ninth page and nothing has happened yet!" said Jiblets.

"I want to leave this book as well!" said Badger.

"Always have done. Ever since that awful front cover."

Sirius scratched his head.

"Well, where would we even go if we left this book?
We could end up in a story with fairies and unicorns and endless line dancing to Belgian Trance.
Or we could be in a story where we're eaten by monsters.

Or we could end up not even being in a book...

Fall off the bookshelf...

And get sucked up by one of those vacuum cleaners!"
said Sirius.

"Stop trying to scare us!" snapped Badger.

"Vacuum cleaners don't exist!"

"Or…"

"We could end up in the

# BEST BOOK EVER!"

cried Jiblets.

"Probably not." said Sirius.

"Well, we want to **leave!**" shouted Jiblets.

"Well, we want to **stay!**" shouted Sirius.

Suddenly… Percy Hogtrotter had an idea.

"Why don't we have a vote?" he said.

They all looked at each other and said, "Good idea!"

It was the fifteenth page and all of the characters were voting on whether to **stay** or **leave** this book.

By the next page all of the votes had been counted, and an exhausted Mayor Gruft declared,

"The result of the vote, shall we all leave or stay in this book is...

# LEAVE!"

"So what do we do now?" asked Sirius, confused.
They all turned to Percy Hogtrotter.

"Don't look at me!" said Percy Hogtrotter,
"I wanted to stay in this book! I'm not sorting this mess out!"

The characters all looked around, wondering what to do.

Hamster stepped forward.
"Fine… I'll sort this out." she said.

"Right," said Hamster, "before we leave this book we have to decide what sort of new book we want to go into. And then we can speak with the author and illustrator."

The characters started shouting their ideas out loud:

"I want to be in a horror story book!"

"A romantic period-drama!"

"Set in the future!"

"With zombies!"

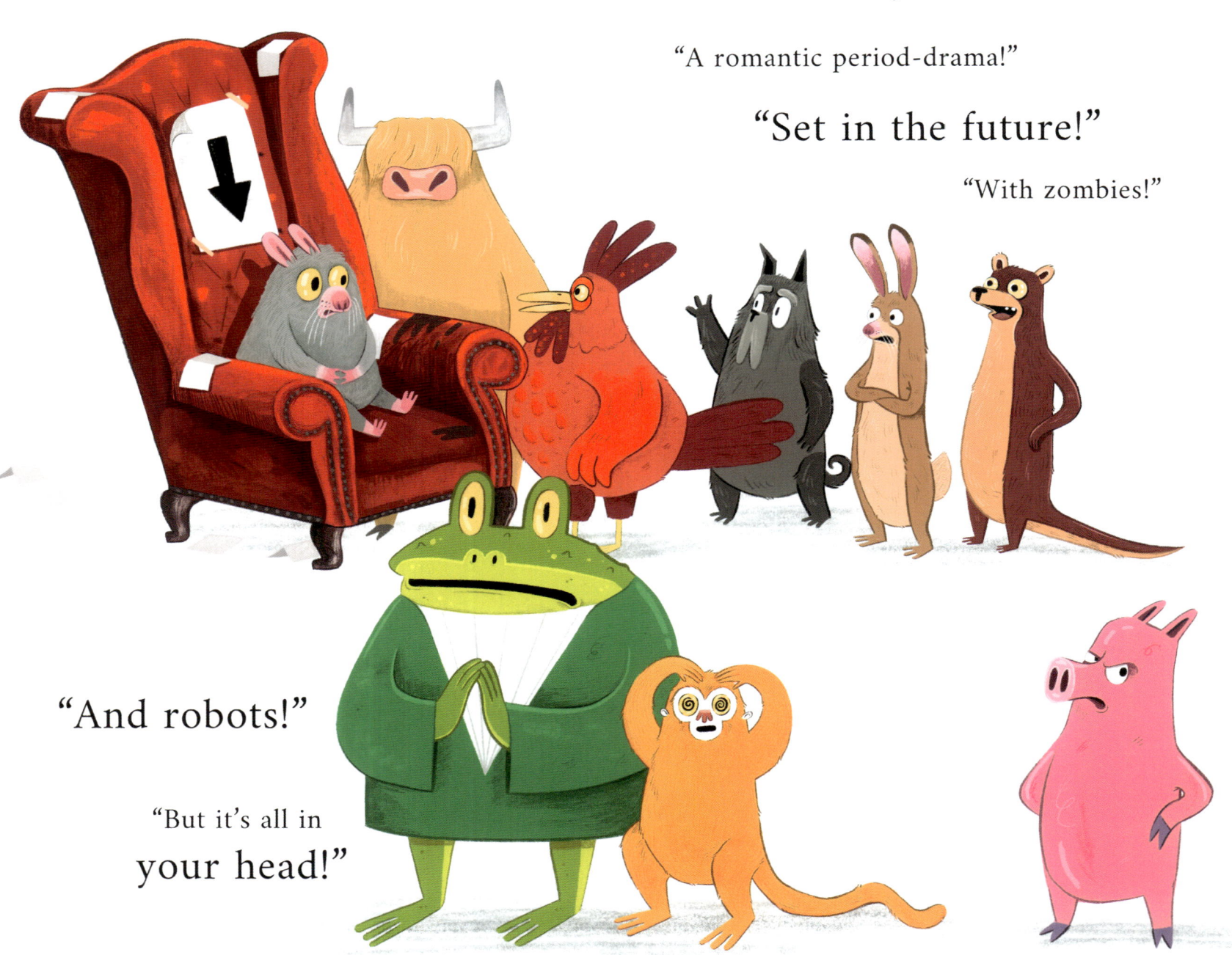

"And robots!"

"But it's all in your head!"

"And the book is just like this!"

"But with bigger pages!"

"And fewer characters!"

Hamster spoke to the author and illustrator and asked that they all move into a
zombie-robot-horror, romantic period-drama,
set in the future,
but it's all in your head.
In a book that looks exactly like this one.
But completely different in every way.

Finally, after lots of discussion, Hamster announced:

"I have made an agreement with the author and illustrator.
On the twenty-second page we're all going to go into a brand new book.
It's a romantic robot period-drama set in the future, with zombie unicorns and it's in a book that pretty much looks like this except all the pages are different sizes.

Oh, and Hen - you have to stay here. It's a comedy."

The characters started complaining.

"I'm not going into that book! It sounds even worse than this one!" moaned Jiblets.

"But I want to stay in this book and be in the story we were supposed to be in before all this started!" shouted the Frog.

"Go back and get us a better book to go into!" shouted Badger.

"It's what you all asked for!" shouted Hamster.
But no one could hear her over the noise of the characters arguing.

The author and illustrator found some extra pages to allow the characters to decide what to do next.

"This is going on **forever!** Look at how much paper we've wasted!" cried Jiblets.

"We could have been coming to the climax of a really, really good story by now… **but no…** we decided to all have a vote and now look at us!" said Sirius.

Once again, the characters began to complain:

"Shall we have another vote?"
"**No!** We had one already and one was one too many!"

"I say we walk off the page. **Right now.**"
"Well whatever we do, we need to do it **together!**"

"I'm not sorting this mess out anymore!" whimpered Hamster.

"Leave it to me!" shouted the Highland Cow, "I've got it!"

"Hey!" he shouted at the author and illustrator.

"We're leaving this book in two pages' time and either you put us in a book we like... Or we'll just make our own book with our own story!"

"What do YOU know about making books?" cried Hen.

"It's only bits of paper and glue." said Badger.

The characters argued...

"I am not leaving this book!" shouted the Rabbit.
"But we all had a vote and we voted to leave!" screamed the Weasel.
"Well let's have another vote!" shouted the Frog.

And **squabbled**...

"Why can't we have that new story but **without** the zombie unicorns?" asked the Pigeon.

"Don't you listen? The author and illustrator said we **have** to have the zombie unicorns or no book!" said Percy Hogtrotter.

"I'm allergic to zombie unicorns." cried the Frog.

And on...

And on...

And on...

In the midst of the characters arguing and squabbling, Sirius and Jiblets found each other.

"I'm sorry!" said Jiblets!

"I'm sorry!" cried Sirius.

"All that matters to me is that I get to be in a story book with you." said Jiblets.

And on the twenty-seventh page of this book, the two best friends hugged and waited for the rabble to die down and for the story to start.

But...

# To be continued...

"Aaaw man! We're still here!"

"Whaaaat? This is never going to end!"

# BREXIT!

IN JUNE 2016, THE BRITISH GOVERNMENT ASKED THE PUBLIC IF THEY WOULD LIKE TO STAY IN THE EUROPEAN UNION. HERE'S WHAT HAPPENED...

## UK

The United Kingdom of Great Britain and Northern Ireland is a sovereign country made up of England, Scotland, Wales and Northern Ireland.

The UK joined the EU in 1973.

## EU

The European Union is a special 'club' for 28 countries from the continent of Europe.

In return for a membership fee, the EU will organise some laws, rules on trade and how people can move from country to country for all the members.

## LEAVE ARGUMENTS

Being in the EU is too expensive and the money could be used on different things.

The EU is making decisions for us that the UK should be making on its own, including:

- What our laws should be.
- Who we are allowed to trade with.
- Who is allowed to come and live and work here.

## REMAIN ARGUMENTS

Being in the EU is far better than being outside:

- Trade between people across Europe is very easy.
- People are able to move around Europe easily.
- Being outside the EU might cause serious money problems for the UK and means we have a lot more work to do on our own.

### WHAT IS A REFERENDUM?

It's a public vote on a very important issue. Anyone who lives in the UK who is over 18 is allowed to vote in a secret ballot.

### 2016 REFERENDUM RESULT

REMAIN 48.1%   LEAVE 51.9%

IT WAS VERY CLOSE!

### WHAT HAPPENS NEXT?

The UK Government need to tell the EU it is leaving (triggering Article 50).

The Government need to work out a deal with the EU on how and when the UK will leave.

# BREXIT TIMELINE

**2016**
- BRITAIN VOTES TO LEAVE THE EU
- PRIME MINISTER DAVID CAMERON QUITS – HE WANTED THE UK TO REMAIN
- THERESA MAY BECOMES THE PRIME MINISTER AND PROMISES TO MAKE THE UK LEAVE THE EU

**2017**
- GOVERNMENT TELLS THE EU IT IS LEAVING IN 2 YEARS
- GENERAL ELECTION SHOCK: THE GOVERNMENT ONLY WIN 318 SEATS OUT OF 650 WHICH MEANS IT WON'T HAVE ENOUGH MPS TO WIN IMPORTANT VOTES ON HOW BREXIT WILL TAKE PLACE

**2018**
- GOVERNMENT DECIDES WHAT SORT OF DEAL IT WILL ASK THE EU TO AGREE TO, INCLUDING DECISIONS ON LAWS, MONEY AND WHAT THE UK WILL TAKE CONTROL OVER AFTER IT LEAVES
- THE UK AND EU CAN'T AGREE ON HOW BREXIT SHOULD HAPPEN, BUT AFTER A LOT OF DISCUSSIONS, THEY FINALLY AGREE A 'DEAL'

**2019**
- THERESA MAY'S 'DEAL' IS REJECTED MULTIPLE TIMES BY MPS WHO VOTE AGAINST IT. THIS MEANS BREXIT WON'T HAPPEN UNLESS A NEW DEAL CAN BE MADE, OR THE UK LEAVES WITH NO DEAL AT ALL
- MPS ARE SO SCARED OF LEAVING THE EU WITH 'NO DEAL' THAT THE GOVERNMENT ASKS THE EU FOR MORE TIME TO DECIDE ON WHAT TO DO NEXT
- THE EU ALLOW THE UK UNTIL 31ST OCTOBER 2019 AT 11PM TO FIND A WAY TO LEAVE
- THERESA MAY FEELS SHE CAN'T HELP THE UK LEAVE THE EU AFTER ALL OF HER EFFORTS, SO SHE QUITS
- BORIS JOHNSON BECOMES THE NEW PRIME MINISTER AND HE PROMISES TO MAKE THE UK LEAVE THE EU BY HALLOWEEN WITH A DEAL OR WITHOUT ONE
- BORIS JOHNSON SPEAKS TO THE EU AND ASKS THEM FOR A NEW 'DEAL' THAT WOULD SUIT THE UK. AFTER LOTS OF TALKS, THEY AGREE
- TIME RUNS OUT ON MPS AGREEING DEAL BEFORE HALLOWEEN, SO THE EU GIVE BRITAIN UNTIL THE END OF JANUARY TO SORT OUT BREXIT
- BECAUSE THE MPS CANNOT AGREE ON BREXIT, THEY DECIDE TO HAVE A GENERAL ELECTION ON 12 DEC

*THIS IS GOING ON FOREVER!*

## WHAT DO ALL THESE WORDS AND PHRASES ACTUALLY MEAN?

# GLOSSARY

**BREXIT:** BRITAIN + EXIT = BREXIT

**MP:** MEMBER OF PARLIAMENT

**PARLIAMENT:** THE UK'S LAWS AND IMPORTANT DECISIONS ARE DECIDED BY A GROUP OF MPS WHO MEET IN THE HOUSE OF COMMONS. THEY VOTE ON WHETHER CERTAIN DECISIONS SHOULD HAPPEN OR NOT. THESE INCLUDE LAWS, HOW MONEY IS SPENT AND, OF COURSE, HOW BREXIT HAPPENS.

**GENERAL ELECTION:** IN A GENERAL ELECTION PEOPLE ALL OVER THE UK GET TO VOTE FOR AN MP TO REPRESENT THEM IN THE HOUSE OF COMMONS. THERE ARE 650 MPS IN TOTAL, EACH REPRESENTING A DIFFERENT PART OF THE UK.

**GOVERNMENT:** TO WIN A GENERAL ELECTION AND FORM A GOVERNMENT, A POLITICAL PARTY MUST WIN OVER 320 SEATS TO HAVE MORE MPS THAN ALL THE OTHER PARTIES PUT TOGETHER. IF THE BIGGEST PARTY DOESN'T HAVE ENOUGH MPS TO FORM A GOVERNMENT, IT IS CALLED A 'HUNG PARLIAMENT'.

**POLITICAL PARTY:** GROUPS OF MPS WHO HAVE SIMILAR IDEAS ON HOW THE COUNTRY SHOULD BE RUN.

**PRIME MINISTER:** THE MP WHO IS IN CHARGE OF THE PARTY WHO FORMS THE GOVERNMENT IS THE PRIME MINISTER. THEY MAKE IMPORTANT DECISIONS.

**"DEAL":** A BREXIT DEAL IS AN AGREEMENT BETWEEN THE UK GOVERNMENT AND THE EU ON HOW THE UK SHOULD LEAVE, WHICH LAWS SHOULD CHANGE, WHICH WILL STAY THE SAME, AND HOW THE UK AND EU WILL WORK TOGETHER AFTER BREXIT. LOTS OF PEOPLE WANT DIFFERENT THINGS FROM A DEAL AND IT IS IMPOSSIBLE TO KEEP EVERYONE HAPPY.

**"NO DEAL":** IF THE GOVERNMENT AND THE EU CAN'T AGREE ON ANYTHING THERE WILL BE NO DEAL. THIS MEANS THE UK LEAVES THE EU WITH LOTS OF LAWS AND IMPORTANT DECISIONS UNDECIDED. MANY PEOPLE ARE WORRIED THIS WOULD CAUSE SERIOUS PROBLEMS BUT OTHERS FEEL IT IS THE ONLY WAY TO LEAVE THE EU.